Fire Engines

by Marcia S. Freeman

Consulting Editor:
Gail Saunders-Smith, Ph.D.

Consultant:
Mark Edelbrock
Fire Fighter
Seattle Fire Department

Pebble Books

an imprint of Capstone Press
Mankato, Minnesota

Pebble Books are published by Capstone Press
818 North Willow Street, Mankato, Minnesota 56001
http://www.capstone-press.com

Library of Congress Cataloging-in-Publication Data
Freeman, Marcia S. (Marcia Sheehan), 1937–
    Fire engines/by Marcia S. Freeman.
    p. cm.—(Community vehicles)
    Includes bibliographical references and index.
    Summary: Illustrations and simple text describe fire engines and the equipment
they carry.
    ISBN 0-7368-0102-2
    1. Fire engines—Juvenile literature. [1. Fire engines.] I. Title. II. Series.
TH9372.F74 1999
628.9'259—dc21   98-18380
                                                                      CIP
                                                                       AC

Note to Parents and Teachers

This series supports national social studies standards related to authority and government. This book describes and illustrates fire engines and the equipment they carry. The photographs support early readers in understanding the text. The sentence structures offer subtle challenges. This book introduces early readers to vocabulary used in this subject area. The vocabulary is defined in the Words to Know section. Early readers may need assistance in reading some words and in using the Table of Contents, Words to Know, Read More, Internet Sites, and Index/Word List sections of the book.

Table of Contents

Fire engines are large trucks. Fire engines carry tools for fighting fires. Fire engines go to fires fast.

Fire engines have sirens and flashing lights. Sirens and lights tell people that fire engines are coming.

Fire engines carry long hoses. Fire fighters hook up hoses to water supplies. Fire fighters use hoses to spray water on big fires.

TO OPERATE
HOLD UPRIGHT — PULL RING PIN
STAND 9 TO 12 FEET FROM FIRE
PRESS LEVER
DIRECT DISCHARGE AT BASE OF
FLAME WITH SIDE TO SIDE MOTION

FOR
△ A
□ B
○ C
FIRES

MODEL TGP 200

General

Fire engines carry
fire extinguishers. Fire
extinguishers spray special
chemicals. Fire fighters
use fire extinguishers to
put out small fires.

Fire engines carry
ladders. The ladders
are different sizes. Fire
fighters use ladders to
reach high places.

Fire engines carry pike poles. Fire fighters use pike poles to tear holes in roofs. The holes let out hot air and smoke.

Fire engines carry big fans. Fire fighters use fans to blow smoke out of rooms. Fires make a lot of smoke.

Fire engines carry air packs. Fire fighters breathe from air packs when there is smoke. Smoke makes air hard to breathe.

Fire engines return to fire stations after fires. Fire fighters clean the fire engines. Fire fighters keep fire engines ready to go to fires.

Words to Know

air pack—a tank of air joined to a mask; fire fighters breathe from air packs when there is a lot of smoke.

fire extinguisher—a holder with water or chemicals inside it; people use fire extinguishers to put out small fires.

hose—a long, bendable tube that carries water from one place to another

ladder—a metal or wood tool that people climb to reach high places

pike pole—a tool with a hook-shaped end used to tear holes in roofs; the holes let out hot air and smoke.

siren—a machine that makes a loud sound

spray—to scatter liquid in fine drops; fire hoses spray water on fires.

Read More

Ready, Dee. *Fire Fighters.* Community Helpers. Mankato, Minn.: Bridgestone Books, 1997.

Saunders-Smith, Gail. *The Fire Station.* Field Trips. Mankato, Minn.: Pebble Books, 1998.

Somerville, Louisa. *Rescue Vehicles.* Look Inside Cross-Sections. New York: Dorling Kindersley, 1995.

Internet Sites

Tour of a Fire Engine
http://www.paonline.com/tdgable/page4a.htm

USFA Kids Homepage
http://www.usfa.fema.gov/kids/index.htm

Why Do Fire Fighters...?
http://www.cybercid.com/lrfd/firefaq.htm

Index/Word List

air, 15, 19
air packs, 19
chemicals, 11
fans, 17
fire extinguishers, 11
fire fighters, 9, 11, 13, 15,
   17, 19, 21
fires, 5, 9, 11, 17, 21
fire stations, 21
holes, 15
hoses, 9

ladders, 13
lights, 7
pike poles, 15
roofs, 15
rooms, 17
sirens, 7
smoke, 15, 17, 19
supplies, 9
tools, 5
trucks, 5
water, 9

Word Count: 184
Early-Intervention Level: 10

Editorial Credits
Colleen Sexton, editor; Clay Schotzko/Icon Productions, cover designer;
   Sheri Gosewisch, photo researcher

Photo Credits
Dembinsky Photo Assoc. Inc., 8; Joe Sroka, cover; Jim Regan, 1; John Mielcarek, 12
Image West/Larry Angier, 18
Mike Heller/911 Pictures, 14, 16, 20
Photo Network/Mark Sherman, 6
Unicorn Stock Photos/Scott Liles, 4; Mike Morris, 10